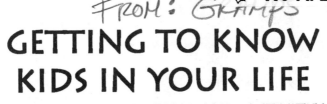

To: Da...
FROM: GRAMPS

W9-AFZ-391

GETTING TO KNOW
KIDS IN YOUR LIFE

INTERACTIVE QUESTIONS AND ACTIVITIES
TO REALLY GET TO KNOW CHILDREN
FOR PARENTS, AUNTS, UNCLES, GRANDPARENTS AND
ANYONE WHO SHARES TIME WITH
3 TO 7 YEAR - OLDS

BY

JEANNE McSWEENEY & CHARLES LEOCHA
WITH DHANA CHESSON

WORLD LEISURE CORPORATION
BOSTON, MA/HAMPSTEAD, NH

Distributed to the trade in U.S.A. by Login Publishers Consortium,
1436 W. Randolph Street, Chicago, IL 60607, tel. (312) 733-8228, (800) 626-4330.
Distributed in Canada by General Publishing Company, Ltd.,
30 Lesmill Road, Don Mills, Ontario, Canada M3B 2T6, tel. (416) 445-3333.
Distributed to gift stores through Sourcebooks, Inc.,
PO Box 372, Naperville, IL 60566, tel. (800) 727-8866, fax (708) 961-2168.
Mail Order and Special Sales by World Leisure Corporation, 177 Paris Street,
Boston MA 02128, tel. (617) 569-1966, fax (617) 561-7654.

ISBN: 0-915009-27-7

INTRODUCTION

Getting to Know Kids in Your Life follows the successful route of interactive questions and activities pioneered in the bestseller *Getting To Know You*, and extends it to focus on children between the ages of 3 and 7.

When you first use this book with children you know, you will be amazed at the enthusiasm generated by your grown-up attention. The answers kids provide are fascinating glimpses into the world as they experience it. You in turn will see your child, grandchild, niece or nephew in quite a different way after you've been through a few of these questions together.

It is easy to say that parents and the extended family should spend time with children, but today's families often find that time is very limited. This small book makes spending your precious time with children as creative, nurturing and enjoyable as possible.

It is in conversation that parents can learn what their children are hearing at school, on the playground and from other adults. Activity between kids and grownups is where values are developed and seasoned.

We all want the children close to us to be happy, well-adjusted, self-confident, and able to relate to and care about others.

These qualities start with us and how much quality time we spend with children in their formative years. These preschool years are some of the most important for development — as well as some of the most delightful to spend with children.

This book is a collection of hundreds of questions and activities that will lead to hundreds more and make the time you spend with children even more special.

These questions have more than "Yes" or "No" answers and
can easily be modified depending on the situation and child.
They will all lead to further discussions.
"Why," "How," or "Tell me more,"
although not spelled out are implied.

When you begin to ask kids questions from this little book
and interact with them through some of these activities,
get ready to experience a new world, as kids see it,
of wonder, delight, exuberance and excitement.

DEDICATION

From Jeanne
To the kids in my life whom I've been lucky enough to get to know and treasure —
Brendan, Rebecca, Trevor and Molly McSweeney — who provide
humorous and helpful insight into the minds and hearts of children.

From Charlie
To Anna and Charlie who provided the inspiration and first real test of this book.

From Dhana: To Gabriel

Special thanks to Audrey McS. Newton,
Directress of Apple Valley Montessori School in Sudbury, MA,
whose multifaceted skills improved this book tremendously.

GETTING TO KNOW
KIDS IN YOUR LIFE

1.

Who is a silly or funny person you know?
Why is he or she silly or funny?

2.

How do you tie a shoe?

3.

If you could play with any character from a fairy tale, who would it be? Why?

4.

What is your favorite ride or activity at an amusement park or fair? Why?

5.

Which holiday do you like the best?
What do you like best about it?

6.

If you could be an animal, which one would you be?
Why?

7.

What do you want to be when you grow up?

8.

What is your favorite food?
How do you make it?

9.

What is your favorite TV show?

10.

Tell me about the silliest thing you ever did.

11.

What is your favorite movie or video?

12.

Do you have an imaginary friend?
What is his or her name?
What do you like to do together?

13.

Do you have something special you sleep with at
night, like a teddy bear or a blanket?

14.

If you could have three wishes, like Aladdin,
what would they be?

15.

Do you know anyone from another country?
Who is that person? Where do they come from?

16.

If you could go anywhere on vacation,
where would it be? Why?

17.

Tell me what you like to do in the car when your
parents are driving.

18.

Do you like to go out to eat?
Where do you like to go?
Tell me what you like about going there.

19.

Have you ever flown in an airplane?
What was the trip like?

20.

Would you rather play outdoors or inside?

21.

Have you ever
ridden on a train?
Where did you go?
What was it like?

22.

What is your favorite dessert?
Tell me what you like best about it.

23.

What is your favorite snack?

24.

How do you get rid of hiccups?

25.

What is your favorite book?

26.

Do you believe in ghosts?
How do you get rid of ghosts
or other scary things?

27.

Do you have to do chores at home? What are they?
Do you like them?

28.

Have you ever gone on a hike? How long was it?
What did you see?

29.

Have you ever been to the country? Big city?
What was your trip like?
What did you see that you liked the most?
Was there anything you didn't like about the trip?

30.

Name three things that make you happy.
Name three things that make you sad.
Name three things that make you angry.

31.

What is your favorite thing to do at home?
At a friend's house?

32.

Do you know your phone number and address?
What are they?

33.

If you were Goldilocks and the Three Bears came
home, what would you do?

34.

If you were Snow White and the Wicked Queen came
to the door and offered you an apple,
what would you do?

35.

What do most people say you are good at doing?

36.

What do you think you are good at doing?

37.

How do you feel when you win?

38.

How do you feel when you lose?

39.

How do you treat other people when they lose to you?

40.

What is your favorite season of the year?
Why is it your favorite?

41.

Have you ever moved or have you always lived in the same place?

42.

Do you have a favorite color? What is it?

43.

Do you know any knock-knock jokes?

44.

What are your favorite things to draw?
Would you draw me pictures of them?

45.

What is your favorite breakfast? Lunch? Dinner?

46.

Do you ever help anyone to cook?
What do you do to help them?

47.

Have you ever taken pictures with a camera?
How did they turn out?
Tell me your favorite things to photograph.
Who showed you how to use the camera?

48.

Do you get an allowance? How much do you get?
What do you have to do to earn your allowance?

49.

Do you have any pets?
What kind? What are their names?

50.

What would you plant in a garden?
Would you rather plant flowers or vegetables?

51.

Name the people in your family. Tell me about them.

52.

Have you ever used a computer?
What do you do or play on it?

53.

Name two friends. How are they the same?
How are they different?

54.

What kind of a party do you want for your next birthday?

55.

When you go to see a movie at a theater, what do you like to eat and drink?

56.

Where do you think babies come from?

57.

Do you play a musical instrument?
What instrument do you play?
What songs can you play on it? Would you like to
play one now? If your answer is no, what instrument
would you like to play? Why?

58.

What was your costume last Halloween?
What will your costume be next time?

59.

Have you ever gotten lost or separated from your parents? Tell me about it.

60.

If you could be a character from the Wizard of Oz, would you choose to be Dorothy, the Cowardly Lion, the Wicked Witch, the Scarecrow, the Tin Man or Toto? Why?

61.

Where do animals in the forest go when it rains?

62.

Can you name your neighbors? What are they like?

63.

How do you get to school in the morning?

64.

How do you get rid of a cold?

65.

Who is your favorite baby-sitter?

66.

What is your teacher like?

67.

If the mailman brought you a letter, who would you want it to come from, and what do you hope the letter would say?

68.

If you were having a party and you could invite any five people in the whole world, who would you invite?

69.

Would you like to be a child forever and not grow up?
Why?

70.

If you could have magical powers,
what would they be?

71.

What does "supercalifragilisticexpialidocious" mean?

72.

When was the last time you saw a rainbow?
Where do rainbows come from?
Would find a pot of gold at the end of a rainbow?

73.

Describe your favorite animal.

74.

What is your favorite kind of cake?

75.

What is your favorite flavor of ice cream?

76.

Where do you go when you want to be alone?

77.

Do you know where eggs come from?
Which came first — the chicken or the egg?

78.

Mickey is a mouse. Donald is a duck. Pluto is a dog.
What is Goofy?

79.

What do you like on your pizza?
How do you make pizza?

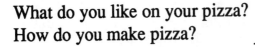

80.

If you were one of the Three Little Pigs and the Big Bad Wolf said he would huff and puff and blow your house down, what would you do?

81.

Have you ever been camping?
Did you sleep in a tent or under the stars?
Did you sleep as well as you do in your own room?
Did you see any bears?

82.

If you were the Ugly Duckling and the other ducks
made fun of you, what would you do?

83.

Why is the sky blue?

(The scientifically savvy adult will know that it's because of
Rayleigh Scattering. You can look this up together in the encyclopedia.)

84.

What is your favorite piece of clothing?

85.

Describe the best present you ever received.

86.

Did you ever get a present you didn't like?
What did you do with it?
Did you tell the person who gave it to you that you
didn't want it?

87.

Name two of your best friends.
Why do you like being with them?

88.

If someone who didn't know your father was looking for him in a store, what would you tell them your father looks like so they could find him?

89.

If someone else was looking for your mother, how would you describe her?

90.

What is your favorite bedtime story?

91.

What is your favorite day of the week?

92.

Do you have a nickname? How did you get it?
Who calls you by your nickname?

93.

Tell me what museums you have visited that were lots
of fun. Why do you like them?

94.

What kinds of things make you cry or upset you?

95.

Is it better to be a girl or a boy? Why?

96.

What does your father do for work?

97.

Tell me your daddy's favorite thing to do.

98.

What is your father's favorite food to eat?

99.

What does your mother do for work?

100.

Tell me your mommy's favorite thing to do.

101.

What is your mom's favorite food to eat?

102.

What is your favorite toy?

103.

What game do you like to play with only one other person?

104.

Tell me about your favorite game to play when you are with a bunch of friends.

105.

Tell me about the last time you had a lot of friends or cousins spend the night with you.
How many people slept over? Where did they all sleep? What did you do to have fun together?
Did you have any pillow fights?

106.

If you were your mommy or daddy, what would you do to make you clean your room?

107.

What does your dad do that you think is weird?

108.

Does your mommy do anything weird?

109.

Where is the all-time best place in your house to hide where nobody can find you?

110.

What food do you dislike the most?
Why don't you like it?

111.

If you could ride on a
flying carpet
where would you go?

112.

When you get up in the morning and your parents are asleep, what is your favorite thing to do that's quiet so you don't wake them up?

113.

Do you know any twins?
Would like to have a twin brother or sister?

114.

Did you ever get angry with your parents? Why?

115.

What happens to the cans and bottles you recycle?

116.

Why is it important to pick up your toys after you are done playing?

117.

Who is a "grownup?"
When will you be a grownup?

118.

If you could be one age for the rest of your life, what age would you like to be?

119.

Do you like riding in boats? Tell me about your last boat ride.

120.

Do things that happen on television and the movies also happen in real life?

Do you think Power Rangers are real? What about the Ninja Turtles? Snow White?
Beauty and the Beast? What's different between TV and real life?

121.

When you grow up, would you rather be very tall or very short or in between?

122.

If someone said a wish would come true if you ate a sandwich full of bugs, would you eat it?

123.

Tell me, what is the nicest thing you remember your mommy doing?

124.

What are some nice things your daddy has done?

125.

What would you do if there was a big rainstorm with thunder and lightning?
What would you do if you saw a tornado coming?
What would you do if there was so much snow you couldn't get out the door?

126.

If you could decide to do anything you wanted to do tomorrow, tell me what it would be.
If you couldn't do that, what would be your second choice?

127.

Do you know what makes thunder and lightning?

128.

Can you tell what kind of animal or bird walked in the snow, in mud, or in sand at the beach from its footprints? How can you tell?

129.

Have you ever told a lie? Why?

130.

Do you think there are little lies and big lies?
Tell me a little lie and a big lie.

131.

If you could go to the jungle, what is the first thing you would do?

132.

What do you like more — going to school during the week or playing on weekends when there's no school?

133.

Tell me about a time when you were so sick you had to stay home in bed.

134.

What cereal do you like best?

135.

What things scare you?

136.

What would it feel like to jump out of a plane with a parachute? Do you think you would ever do it?

137.

If you had to eat the same food every day for a whole week, breakfast, lunch and dinner, what would you want it to be?

138.

If your parents had to eat the same food every day for a whole week, what would you pick for them to eat?

139.

Do people ever tell you that you can't do something because you aren't big enough yet?
How does that make you feel?

140.

If you could be beautiful, strong or smart, which one would you choose?

141.

Do you know
how to swim?
Who taught you?
Do you want
to learn?

142.

Can you do any gymnastics like tumbling, somersaults or cartwheels?
Have you ever jumped on a trampoline?

143.

Would you still brush your teeth every night before going to sleep if your parents didn't make you? Why?

144.

Why do you think some people have different color skin? Do you have any friends whose skin is a different color from yours?

145.

What do people like best about you?

146.

What are good table manners?
Do you know anyone who does not have good table manners?

147.

If a new kid came into your class or neighborhood, how would you make them feel comfortable?

148.

Do you think you can talk to animals?
Would you like to?
What kind of animal would you like to talk to be able to talk to?
What would you ask it?

149.

How does the Tooth Fairy know you lost a tooth?

150.

Have you ever seen grownups dancing?
Do you like dancing? What is your favorite dance?
Who is your favorite dance partner?

151.

Is there anything that you used to be afraid of that doesn't scare you any more?

152.

Would you like to have another brother or sister? Would you want them to be older or younger than you?

153.

Do you have a lot of cousins? Can you name them? Who are your favorite cousins?

154.

Do you ever let someone else win a game if you know they will cry if they lose?

155.

Tell me about the worst nightmare you ever had. How did you go back to sleep?

156.

Tell me the best dream you ever had.

157.

What is the worst program on television?

158.

If you could pick a new first name,
what would you choose?

159.

If you could look into a magic mirror like Belle in Beauty and the Beast, what would you ask to see?

160.

Tell me about the nicest person you know. Who is the meanest person you know?

161.

Have you ever seen a grownup cry?
Why were they crying? How did it make you feel?

162.

Which is better — playing at your house or at your friend's house?

163.

What is the smallest animal in the world?
What is the biggest animal?
What would you do every day if you were one of
these animals?

(The well-prepared adult may wish to have a copy of the *Guinness Book of World Records* at hand for questions like these.)

164.

What do you like doing best at school?

165.

If you were going on a trip and could take only one thing — what would it be?

166.

Should you share your toys with your friends when they come to your house to play?
Do you have any toys you will never share?

167.

Name something you don't like about school.

168.

If your parents went on a long trip and you could live with someone else for a month, who would you like to live with? Would you like to go live in their house, or have them come live with you?

169.

Have you ever gone horseback riding?
Would you like to? Why?
What was it like? What was the horse's name?
What color was your horse?

170.

Tell me the worst thing you ever smelled.

171.

What is something you do that you know will make your parents angry?
What do you do that makes them happy?

172.

What are your grandparents like?

173.

When you're sad, what do you do to make
yourself happy?
If someone wanted to make you happy what would
you like them to do?

174.

Have you ever traveled to another country?

175.

If someone gave you $10, what would you do with it?

176.

Tell me what you would like to learn more than anything else in the world.

177.

Can you make any sounds like animals?
Make some sounds and I'll guess what animal it is.

178.

When you go to a zoo what is your
favorite animal to visit?

179.

Have you ever been
to an aquarium?
What is your favorite fish?

180.

What do you think clouds are made of?

181.

Would you like to be a bird? Why?
What kind of bird would you like to be?

182.

How does it make you feel when people
hug and kiss you?

183.

Do you know how to sing any songs?
O.K., let me hear one.

184.

What kinds of bugs have you seen?
What is the biggest bug you ever saw?

185.

Who do you think is the smartest person in the world?

186.

What do you think is the strongest animal in the world?

187.

If you could take a trip to the moon, tell me what you think it would be like up there.

188.

Are there any smells you really like — such as when a cake is baking, or your parents are cooking dinner, or your mommy's perfume?

189.

Most people have cats and dogs for pets —
Which do you like better?
What other kinds of pets do people have?
What kind of animal wouldn't make a good pet?
Why?

190.

Do you think fish can hear? Why?
How do they hear? They don't have any ears.

191.

What is the longest trip you ever went on?

192.

What sorts of things do you like to do during the
winter? What about summer, spring and fall?

193.

What do you think it
would be like to be a
snake and not have any
arms or legs?

194.

I'll bet you are a good artist. Would you draw a picture for me? What is your favorite thing to draw?

195.

Do you like to play with just one favorite toy, or would you rather play with a lot of toys?

196.

Have you ever played in snow?
What is the best thing about snow?

197.

What sports do you like to watch?
Which ones do you like to play?

198.

What is your favorite fruit? Your favorite vegetable?

199.

Do you have more fun when you are playing with girls or boys?

200.

What makes boys and girls different?
How are they the same?

201.

Why do you think girls wear dresses and and skirts?
Are there countries where boys wear skirts?

ACTIVITIES

These activities are designed to increase
communication between grownup and child.
They require both of you to do something together—
you have to interact.
There is no better way to get to know children,
and have them get to know you.

1.

Make finger, hand or foot prints on big sheets of paper. Let them dry and then add features with markers to make creatures.

2.

Take a trip on public transportation.

Go for an adventure and ride on several different types of public transportation. Try as many as you can —
subways, buses, ferries,
trains, streetcars . . .

3.

Go pick fruit or vegetables, then prepare something
together with what you picked.

Everywhere in the country there are orchards and farms where you can
go with children to pick fruits and vegetables. If you live in a city,
you will find these farms and orchards only a short drive away.

4.

Read a story about a local historic figure or event, then go on a tour of where history took place.

For instance, in Boston you might read about the Midnight Ride of Paul Revere; in Pennsylvania about Washington's winter in Valley Forge; in Texas about the Alamo; in California, Sutter's Mill and the Gold Rush days.

5.

First read about an activity or animal, then go to a
museum, zoo, aquarium or airport and see the
real thing.

Read a book about how an airport works, then visit an airport tower or
observation deck.

Read about animals on the African Serengeti, then see them in the zoo.

Read about diving under the sea and visit an aquarium.

6.

Go on a factory tour. Show the kids how candy, tires, potato chips, cars, glass, and such are made.

For instance, go to:
- Ben & Jerry's Ice Cream factory in Waterbury, VT
- Binney & Smith in Easton, PA — home of Crayola crayons
- The Lionel Train factory in Mt. Clemens, MI
- Herman Goelitz, home of Jelly Belly beans, in Fairfield, CA

A good source for places near you: *Watch it Made in the U.S.A.* by Brumberg and Axelrod, John Muir Press; $16.95.

7.

Visit an outdoor market together.

Head out to any type of market — flea market, vegetable market, yard sale, etc. They all generate plenty of conversations.

8.

Visit a farm and see cows being milked, and hens laying eggs.

9.

Go to a puppet show or storytelling together.

10.

Cook something together. First use a cookbook with pictures to pick out something that looks good and then prepare it together.

You can combine this with a trip to an outdoor fruit and vegetable market or a trip to pick fruit or vegetables.

11.

Tell stories. You don't have to make them up.
Tell your kids about your first day at school, your old
friends, a trip you went on, a time you were scared.
Tell them about what their grandparents were like as
parents or relate funny stories about aunts and uncles.

12.

Go outside and pick out shapes in the clouds together. Then read or talk together about how clouds are made.

You can try to guess the weather by looking at the clouds. A teakettle can help show how clouds are formed and how rain is made. Besides picking out shapes in the clouds, teach children about the different types of clouds—cirrus, cumulus and stratus. Go to a library or nature book store to find a book on clouds, or use an encyclopedia.

13.

Make a list of good deeds — how to be kind to other people. You might start with how to be kind to specific people such as teachers, friends, grandparents, baby-sitters, or brothers and sisters.

14.

Go on a picnic and let the children choose the menu and help prepare the food.

15.

Play a game of I Spy. "I spy with my two eyes . . ."

There are many variations of this game. All are great fun with this age
group. Pick out something in the room (a blue book for instance)
and say, "I spy with my two eyes something blue I read to you."
Then the child guesses what you are describing.
Continue taking turns with this game.

16.

Read about a foreign country and then go out
together to try their national food.
Try Chinese, Italian, Mexican, Indian, Middle
Eastern, Spanish or others in your neighborhood.
If it is impossible to find any nearby, try cooking up
some foreign recipes at home.

17.

Make a volcano with baking soda and vinegar.

When vinegar and baking soda are mixed, foam is created. Try pouring some vinegar on baking soda in a coffee mug to test the reaction. Use your imagination to create a volcano.

18.

Go kite flying together.

Combine it with a discussion of wind.
Try to guess the wind speed. Look for flags or wind vanes so you can guess the direction of the wind.
Watch birds floating on the wind. For more ideas read *The Kids' Nature Book* by Susan Milord.

19.

I want my Mummy — let your kids wrap you up in toilet paper. First talk with them and show them pictures about Egypt, the Pyramids and mummies.

If there is a group of children, they can choose a mummy and work to wrap him or her. Or several teams of mummy wrappers can compete to make the best mummy. Tell them the toilet paper is old, delicate mummy wrapping from Egypt. Music (Egyptian if you can find it . . . maybe spooky) adds to the mood.

20.

Set up a scavenger hunt.

You can do this as a team or with a group of children. Each child or team takes off with a paper bag and has to find specific items. If the children can read, try making a list, but for 4 to 7 year-olds it is best to send them out to scavenge for one item at a time or do it together. For instance, look for a dead leaf, a seed, a feather, a smooth stone, a twig, something red, or a piece of bark.

21.

Play world or U.S. map games.

Where do you live? Where was your mommy born? Where is it hot? Where's California? Where's France? Where did Hercules come from? Perhaps identify friends who come from other parts of the world, or other parts of the country.

22.

At night point out stars and make up stories about them. Explain what stars are and perhaps point out the easily identified constellations.

23.

Read books and stories to your children regularly. They ask hundreds of questions and you have to interact.
Help a child get a library card in their own name and go to the library together every couple of weeks.

24.

Buy pumpkins and make one happy face and one scary face, then make a pie or roast the pumpkin seeds.

25.

Go to the beach and look for seaweed, starfish, different kinds of shells and other seashore discoveries.

26.

Take a trip back in time, explaining to the kids how it used to be. Take them to an antique shop or a restored village. Show them record players, typewriters, old TVs, and other, even older, devices.

27.

Go on a bug hunt and make a terrarium.

28.

Play games to develop observation skills.

Walk down a street and then ask, "What did you see?"
Ask children to physically describe a person. A good way to do this is
to have them look at you and then turn their back and describe you.
You should try it too. Observation games can be done with little things.
Every child can recognize their own dog or cat — try giving them
their own pet bean or peanut, let them examine it closely, and then let
them try to pick it out from a half-dozen beans or peanuts.

29.

Help children develop a sense of direction by walking together to the store or a nearby friend's house and then having the child direct you home.
Try this game while driving — you drive to your destination and ask the child to direct you back home.

30.

Go for a hike or nature walk together and look for
neat things you can use to make something
(bird house, leaf collage, wreath, a feather pen).

There is a great book dedicated to these activities—
EcoArt by Laurie Carlson, Williamson Publishing Co.

31.

Explore the world of trees. Find a fallen tree, cut off
the end with a saw and count the rings. From that
dead tree's size try to guess the ages of living trees.
Identify trees (start with the difference between leafy
trees and pine trees).

Look for these books to help with any nature activity —
The Original Backyard Scientist by Jane Hoffman
The Kids' Nature Book by Susan Milord, Williamson Publishing Co.

32.

Plant an herb garden with your child in your yard or a window box. (Use these herbs when you and your child cook.)

33.

Participate together in a community cleanup.
Team this up with a trip to a recycling center or a
discussion of recycling and trash.

For more activites and specifics check out Claudia Jones's books,
Parents Are Teachers, Too and *More Parents Are Teachers, Too*
Williamson Publishing Co.

34.

Take your child to work with you and
show them what you do.

35.

Go to a craft fair. You can often see things being made by artisans working in their booths.

36.

Make a world animal map with pictures of animals you find on different continents. Either draw or color the animals or use stickers to put them in the right places.

37.

Raise a butterfly. You can buy a monarch caterpillar in a pet store and then raise it on milkweed until it cocoons and emerges!

38.

Go to a butterfly sanctuary. It's an experience both you and kids will remember for a long time. There are a few great ones in each area of the country as well as several excellent sanctuaries at many zoos.

39.

Put up a bird or hummingbird feeder and try to identify birds that come to eat by your window. Use a bird guide to help identify which birds come to the feeder. Do different birds come in winter and summer?

40.

Wildflower pressing or four-leaf clover hunt. Press them or make a chain or flower crowns and bracelets.

Check out one of the books in your library dealing with nature arts and crafts. There are books on pressing flowers, decorating with pine cones and flower petals, making wreaths, rubbing leaves and bark, and much more.

41.

Go on a nature walk and learn to use a compass.

42.

Learn easy magic tricks together and perform your own little magic show.

43.

Learn about a holiday they have in another country or a different holiday your family doesn't celebrate. (Kwanza, Cinco de Mayo, Carneval) Or make up your own holidays and celebrate them.

44.

Make a "Me in the World" collage. Together with your child, cut pictures from old magazines, catalogs and junk mail that represent things your child likes or wants to do, and make a collage.

45.

Together, plant a flowering garden with bushes and flowers that bloom throughout the growing season. The entire process is a learning experience —

 discovering the differences between seeds and bulbs and planning the times of your blossoms.

46.

Play games together that you used to play as a kid —
hopscotch, pick up sticks, jacks, dominoes, Chinese
checkers, and Chinese or Double Dutch jump rope.

47.

Learn sign language. Check out a book of sign language from the library and learn some real signs, then make up secret signs you can use with each other.

48.

Investigate and make a family tree with pictures of your family.

49.

Make a calendar. Mark kid's activities and grownup's activities so you each know what the other is doing.

If you make a calendar showing your activities and match it with a calendar of a child's activities, children can learn what you do during the day and be able to relate it to what they are doing at the same time.

50.

Write a letter together to your congressman or the President or someone else who will respond (celebrity, movie star, or athlete).

Or send for free stuff from the Government Printing Office or tourist boards. Go to the post office and buy stamps together to send the letter.

Look for *Free Stuff for Kids*, Meadowbrook Press.

51.

For holidays make homemade cards and wrapping paper rather than buying them.

52.

Play a game of Twenty Questions.

This game, played with Yes and No questions, teaches children to think and consider characteristics of items.

Start with general questions (Is it an animal? Is it a piece of furniture? Is it a plant?) to narrow down the category, then move to more specific qualities (Is it in this room? Is it blue? Is it wet?).

53.

Tell add-on stories or chain stories with kids.

These are stories where one person starts the tale and then the other adds on the next situation. This activity can involve two or more participants.

Person #1: It was a dark and stormy night.

Person #2: Jenny was walking home after school

Person #1: It had been a hard day at school. Jenny just got her report card.

Person #2: She didn't want to show it to her mother . . .

Stay in touch

We hope you enjoyed this book. Working with children can be
one of life's most rewarding endeavors.
If you have any ideas for questions or activities to include
in a new edition please send them to:

Getting To Know Kids
World Leisure Corporation
P.O. Box 160
Hampstead, NH 03841

THE AUTHORS

Jeanne McSweeney, co-author of *Getting To Know You*, is still a kid
masquerading as an author, marketing executive and college instructor.
She's one of the few adults who has no complaints about her childhood
because her parents, brothers and sister listened to her
and went the extra mile to get to know her.

Charlie Leocha, the other half of the *Getting To Know You* team,
still believes in magic, unsuppressed imagination, nurturing a child's dreams
(even when the child is 45), and diving passionately into as much of life as possible.
He makes a mean fort from couch cushions with his niece and nephew.

Dhana Chesson still manages to see life from from a kid's perspective.
Between studies and coaching children's soccer she trains for the running of the
bulls in Pamplona. She's not sure where she'll settle, if ever,
but you'll probably find her near a Spanish bar or in some other warm clime.